Legal Basics for Teachers

by
Robert L. Monks
and
Ernest I. Proulx

Library of Congress Catalog Card Number 85-63690
ISBN 0-87367-235-6
Copyright © 1986 by the Phi Delta Kappa Educational Foundation
Bloomington, Indiana

This fastback is sponsored by the Louisville Kentucky Chapter of Phi Delta Kappa, which made a generous contribution toward publication costs.

The chapter sponsors this fastback in memory of Charles E. Sanders (1908-1984), an advocate of and diligent participant in educational excellence in Kentucky's schools.

Table of Contents

Introduction

This fastback presents, in nontechnical language, some basic guidelines for teachers, which if observed will minimize the possibility of lawsuits resulting from incidents occurring in school settings.

Legislators enact legislation, but judges and juries interpret that legislation when they hear the facts presented in lawsuits filed against teachers. Interpretations are influenced by subjective factors; therefore, different interpretations by different judges are often rendered in cases where the facts seem quite similar. The guidelines set forth in this fastback are based on trends in court decisions rather than on any hard and fast rules. While some generalizations have been made, the reader should keep in mind that teachers' actions also are affected by state laws, local school board policies, and building regulations.

In preparing these guidelines we have used legal precedent, research, and our own experiences as a school administrator and as a director of student teaching. Our intent is not to provide a definitive treatment of school-related legal issues but rather to alert teachers to actions in their classroom or while supervising extracurricular activities that could lead to a lawsuit. A short bibliography is provided for those readers who would like to read more about the subject or are interested in case citations.

No advice presented in this fastback is meant to minimize the importance of legal counsel should a school-related legal problem occur. Our purpose is to suggest teacher behaviors that will strengthen the teacher's position before and after an incident occurs.

Some Basic Terminology

This section includes definitions and a brief discussion of legal terms dealing with liability when misfortunes happen to children in school.

Pure Accident. Most accidents in school are "pure" accidents and no one is liable. Even with the best supervision, a child playing catch could be injured by an errant ball. In a gymnastics class, even with proper supervision, instruction, spotters, and adequate equipment, a student could fall the wrong way and break a collarbone. Again, as a pure accident, no one is liable.

Contributory Negligence. This refers to those situations in which the injured party contributed to the accident by doing something he should not have done. For example, in a shop where a student is provided safety glasses and is specifically instructed by the teacher to wear them but fails to do so and is struck in the eye by a wood chip, then the student "contributed" to the accident by not wearing the provided glasses.

Comparative Negligence. This refers to those situations in which the injured party contributed to the injury by doing something he was told not to do, but the accident occurred because of an unsafe condition in the school. The following is an example of comparative negligence: A stairway railing is loose but the school administrator did not have it fixed. A student runs down the stairs, even though all running in the school is prohibited by school rules. The running student leans against the loose rail; it collapses, and the student falls and breaks his arm. If this injury results in a lawsuit, the judge would have to ascertain the comparative liability of each party and make a decision based on that judgment.

Assumption of Risk. Many school activities are inherently dangerous. A student could be burned in a home economics class or cut while doing linoleum block carving in an art class. A variety of accidents can occur in physical education classes. Students assume some risk by participating in any class activity. But if the instruction is appropriate, the equipment is adequate, and an accident occurs, it is not likely the teacher will be found liable. However, the student does not assume any risk if the instruction is inappropriate or the equipment is inadequate. For example, if a football player is issued a cracked helmet and as a result suffers brain damage in blocking practice or a game, the student did not assume the risk. With proper equipment the same accident could have occurred, but in that case the pure-accident principle would prevail. With the cracked helmet, the coach and the school would most likely be liable.

Attractive Nuisance. This refers to conditions in a classroom or work station that attract students but at the same time present a potential danger. A few examples will make this concept clearer.

In some schools during passing periods students use the gymnasium to get from one area of the building to the other. When students walk through the gymnasium and observe a trampoline unfolded, a climbing rope hanging, or flying rings dangling, they often are attracted to jump on the trampoline, climb the rope, or swing on the rings. If no teacher is present — which is often the case during a passing period — and a student gets hurt, the school could be found liable. If students have to pass through the gymnasium, then the teacher should see that the trampoline is folded and the ropes and rings pulled up and inaccessible. While this may seem to be an unnecessary and a time-consuming chore, it will all but eliminate the possibility of a student getting hurt on an attractive nuisance.

Some schools have swimming pools. If students wander into an unattended pool area, they might lean down to feel the water temperature or engage in horseplay around the pool. In either case, a student could fall into the water and drown. Some courts have found an unlocked pool area to be an attractive nuisance. When no formal class is being held at the pool, the doors to the pool area must be locked.

Another example is the chemistry classroom where chemicals are not kept under lock and key. Some students might open bottles of chemicals, smell them or mix them, and an injury results. All chemicals should be locked in storage cabinets. The failure to observe such protective measures could lead to a charge of maintaining an attractive nuisance.

In a school for the mentally handicapped, which the authors visited, the audiovisual equipment — 16mm projectors, overhead projectors, and opaque projectors — was stored on the top shelf of open cabinets. This was done purposely to keep the equipment out of reach of the students. However, the cabinets were not fastened to the wall. A curious student might attempt to reach the equipment by climbing the shelves and the entire cabinet could topple, resulting in injury to the student. In this situation, it is likely that a court would rule that the teacher had maintained an attractive nuisance.

Every teacher should examine his or her classroom or work station to determine if there is anything that is potentially dangerous and likely to attract students. If so, then steps must be taken to remedy the situation.

Reporting Child Abuse

A day seldom passes without the local news media reporting some form of child abuse. Child abuse has become a national concern. Laws in all 50 states require the reporting of suspected child abuse. And since teachers have contact with children each day, most state laws or school codes mandate that teachers report suspected child abuse. (See fastback 172 *The School's Role in the Prevention of Child Abuse*.)

The language of such laws or codes is quite specific. It says the teacher *must* report, not *may* report. Thus, if the teacher suspects child abuse and does not report it, the teacher is probably in violation of state law. Further, the language refers to *suspected* child abuse; it does not say that the teacher must know for certain that abuse has occurred.

The reporting process will vary from district to district. In some districts the teacher reports to the principal. In others the teacher reports the suspected abuse to the school social worker. It is rare for a school district to have a policy whereby the teacher communicates directly with the welfare department.

Some state laws or school codes specify examples of child abuse. Such lists might include malnutrition, physical abuse, lack of proper clothing, lack of dental care, and incest, among others.

Finally, most state laws or school codes provide immunity from slander or libel suits when a teacher reports suspected child abuse or testifies in court against a parent or guardian. This immunity provision relieves teachers from any anxiety they might have about reporting suspected child abuse.

Self-Defense

Self-defense is broadly defined here to include those actions that a teacher takes to defend himself or herself against a student threatening bodily harm, to inhibit a student from inflicting injury on another student, and to stop a student from damaging or destroying school property.

A general guide for teachers when self-defense is necessary is the "use of reasonable force." If the teacher acts reasonably and if a student injury results, courts tend to uphold the teacher. If two students are fighting and if the teacher dislocates a student's shoulder while separating the combatants, a court will probably not find the teacher liable for the injury.

If a teacher uses unnecessary or unreasonable force, courts will not support the teacher's action. In one case a seventh-grade male student who weighed 110 pounds struck the teacher. The teacher, a 220-pound coach, grabbed the student, lifted him off the ground and threw him against the wall, breaking the student's back. When the parents sued the teacher, the teacher offered a plea of self-defense. In this case the teacher was found guilty of battery because the court did not feel the teacher used reasonable force.

A distinction needs to be made here between assault and battery. Assault has come to mean a *threat* to do harm. The teacher's reaction to such threats should be tempered by the seriousness of the threat and the ability of the person who is making it actually to carry it out. If a third-grade child threatens to "get" the teacher after school, the threat is not likely to be carried out and the teacher should not over-react. On the other hand, if a high school student threatens to slash a teacher's automobile tires, the student probably can fulfill the threat. In this instance the teacher should report the threat to the proper school authority for disciplinary action. Too often threats to teachers' person or property are not taken seriously and reported unless the student takes some overt action. We feel that if threats are reported and proper disciplinary action taken, there will be a decrease in harm to teachers or to their property.

Battery refers to an unlawful attack on another. To be guilty of battery, a person must wantonly and willfully harm another. There have been cases in which a teacher filed charges against a student who unintentionally bumped the teacher in the hallway. Incidents of this kind usually do not result in charges of battery being sustained. Battery is usually sustained in cases where it is accompanied by assault — a threat to do harm.

No teacher should accept physical abuse from students. The teacher should either report the student to the appropriate administrator and seek disciplinary action or file legal charges against the student. Failure to report threats because of fear of student reprisals only tends to foster further teacher abuse.

In summary, in a threatening situation that calls for self-defense, the teacher must act reasonably and not use excessive force in handling a disruptive or hostile student.

Possession and Use of Controlled Substances

T eachers and administrators have the responsibility of keeping controlled substances (drugs, alcohol) out of the school but also have the responsibility of respecting students' constitutional rights. The first step should be a school board policy, widely promulgated to students, which prohibits the possession or use of controlled substances in the school. Such a policy forms the basis for teacher action. Thus, if a teacher or administrator suspects or knows that a student is selling or is in possession of controlled substances, the student may be searched and any controlled substance confiscated. Courts have tended to uphold this kind of teacher action, reasoning that teachers are acting *in loco parentis* as long as they act as a reasonable and prudent parent would act.

A problem arises, however, when school personnel search all students. Generally, searches of this kind have not been upheld by the courts. Also, school disciplinary action toward a student who has been charged in court with the possession or use of controlled substances *outside of school* will probably not be upheld in court.

The use or possession of tobacco in the school presents a different problem. For safety and health reasons school officials may establish a policy prohibiting smoking on the school property. If students violate the policy, they may receive disciplinary action, including expulsion. The problem arises when school officials establish policies that prohibit the possession of tobacco in the school. Possession of cigarettes by minors in the United States has become an accepted way of life. Teachers should therefore proceed cautiously before confiscating cigarettes when a student is only carrying them and not smoking them on school property. Courts have tended to shy away from cases involving possession of cigarettes; therefore, no legal precedent is available.

Privileged Communication

Legal issues involving privileged communication focus around two questions: First, can a teacher relate to a third party defamatory information about a student? Second, is information provided to a teacher by a student privileged? That is, can a teacher be required to communicate that information by a court subpoena?

With respect to the first question, the guiding principle is that defamatory remarks about students should only be transmitted to those who have a reason to know, such as a guidance counselor who has the student as a client, or the school administrator or social worker. In sending records to another school to which the student has transferred, only factual information should be transmitted, not rumors, hearsay, or other unsubstantiated information.

Most states have laws that protect the confidentiality of student records. Teachers should become familiar with such laws. We also suggest that any request for personal information be submitted in writing. On receipt of the written request, the teacher should take steps to confirm that the request is valid and that the student or parent has given permission for the request. Only after taking these steps should information about a student be released. These suggestions are based on Section 1 of the federal Family Rights and Privacy Act. Some states have adopted their own student-records acts that relate to this point.

With respect to the second question, teachers must remember that even though the students tell them confidential information, the teacher does not enjoy the same status relating to privileged communication as does a physician, attorney, or a priest in the confessional. Sometimes students regard a likeable teacher as a confidant with whom they can share indiscretions, fears, and other personal information. Even if teachers accept this role and assure students they will not breach their confidence, under certain court orders the teacher might be required to relate confidential information about a student. Whether a school counselor can be mandated by a court to relate information received from a student/client is unclear. The trend of legal decisions supports the principle that the counselor/client relationship is privileged.

Administering First Aid and Medication

Often teachers administer first aid or are requested to give medication to students. Both of these actions have been the basis of a number of suits against teachers in recent years. Teachers have been held liable for acts of omission as well as acts of commission. Observance of guidelines suggested below will benefit teachers should they be sued over an incident related to administering first aid or medication.

First Aid

Two guidelines to follow when administering first aid are: First, perform only such first aid as necessary to save life or limb. Most injuries that happen in school do not fall into this category. Second, act as a prudent parent would act under similar circumstances. Obviously, if a student cuts himself or is choking the teacher must act in accord with his or her training and understanding of accepted practices in such emergencies. Preferably, the teacher should see that the student gets immediate professional care. However, if such care is not available, then the teacher must take reasonable action. After applying emergency first aid, a medical report should be filed with the principal, the parent notified, and professional medical care sought.

Dislocated shoulders or fingers or minor burns are not life or limb endangering injuries. In these instances the teacher should make the student as comfortable as possible and follow local school policy in notifying the parent and seeking professional medical care. A review of case law indicates a number of instances in which teachers have been found liable for attempting to relocate a shoulder and causing permanent damage. Instances also have occurred in which teachers were found liable for applying ointment to a burn, only to discover that the student is allergic to the ointment and a serious medical problem resulted. In the case of a scraped knee, the safest course for a teacher is simply to wash the wound with water. Again, the teacher should approach each situation with the question, "What would a prudent parent do under the same circumstances?"

Medication

A general guideline is that the teacher should give no medication to students. However, there are some circumstances that necessitate the teacher giving medication to students or allowing students to take medication. If there is no school nurse on duty and a student needs to take medication periodically during the school day, the teacher may have to assume the responsibility to see that the student does so. In such cases the teacher should not accept a parent's note or phone call giving directions for frequency and dosage, because they may be unclear or inaccurate. The teacher must see the doctor's prescription to make sure the directions are followed precisely. Also, some medications must be refrigerated; the teacher might not know this without actually seeing the prescription.

If a student asks permission to take medication, the teacher should ask to see the doctor's prescription. Of course, some students will go to the restroom and self-administer medication without the teacher's knowledge. In such cases, the teacher cannot be held liable.

Finally, the teacher should not give students nonprescription medications such as cough drops, cough syrup, aspirin, etc. Such items could contain stimulants that are harmful to students with heart conditions. Nor should teachers give insulin shots. If they are needed during the school day, then the parent should come to school to give the injection or arrange for some other non-school person to give the injection.

In conclusion, our guideline is that teachers give no medication. This is the job of the school nurse. In the absence of the school nurse or if an emergency situation exists, the teacher should follow the suggestions above.

Conducting Field Trips

Teachers often plan field trips to supplement classroom instruction. While field trips have long been used for curriculum enrichment, they do present liability issues for teachers. Observance of the guidelines suggested below will lessen the chances of lawsuits occurring as a result of incidents on a field trip.

Parent Permission Forms

Prior to any field trip the teacher should obtain from each student a permission form signed by a parent or guardian. Under no circumstances should the teacher accept a phone call in lieu of the signed permission form. If an accident occurs, the parent can deny having talked with the teacher. This form should indicate the date, location, and mode of transportation. We also advise including a statement that the parent absolves the teacher and the school from liability should an accident occur. This liability statement is helpful in court if an accident occurs and a parent brings suit, but it does not protect the teacher or school if there were negligence.

In the absence of such a signed form, the student should not be allowed to go on the field trip. Arrangements should be made for the student to stay at school for the duration of the normal school day.

Adequate Supervision

Teachers can reduce the possibility of liability on field trips by making sure there is an adequate number of adult supervisors. What is adequate will depend on the circumstances. Taking a group of students to a local bank would not require as many supervisors as taking the same group to a local steel mill. When deciding on the number of adult supervisors, a teacher should consider the age of the students, type of students (for example, special education), number of past discipline problems in the class, and the nature of the facility to be visited.

We suggest that a "buddy" system be set up before leaving the school. The world is full of strange people. A student should not visit a public restroom alone.

A behavior code should be sent to the home before the trip so parents can review expected behavior with their children. It is also important for students to understand what is appropriate behavior on a field trip. Finally, students should be advised as to procedures to follow should they get separated from the group.

Supervision by Invitee and Licensee

Related to supervision is the issue of how much responsibility for supervision of students rests on the institution being visited. This will depend on whether the student group is an *invitee* or *licensee*. If the institution offers tours, sends letters to teachers, or in some other way encourages teachers to bring students to its facility, the class is considered an invitee and the major responsibility for supervision falls on the institution. Under invitee conditions, it is reasonable to expect the institution to provide tour guides, safety goggles if necessary, and other appropriate safety measures. On the other hand, if the teacher seeks permission to visit a facility and permission is granted, the class is a licensee. Under this condition, the institution is expected to provide only minimal supervision. As a licensee, it would behoove the teacher to discuss with the institutional representative the suggested number of supervisors and other matters related to student behavior and safety.

Transportation

The teacher must ensure that safe and appropriate transportation is available for field trips. It is best to use school-owned or hired buses. Although it may sometimes be necessary to use private automobiles, we strongly discourage this practice since the teacher and the school could be liable for the acts of its agents, the drivers.

Before the trip students should be informed about appropriate behavior while on the bus. A student should never be put off the bus en route for inappropriate behavior. Disciplinary measures can be administered back at school on completion of the field trip.

We further suggest that students be assigned seats on the bus. Even though students may not like assigned seats, the procedure is useful in controlling student behavior; if every student is in an assigned seat, it is easy to determine if someone is missing when it is time to leave.

In conclusion, we emphasize the necessity of thorough pre-trip planning, adequate supervision while on the trip, and proper and safe transportation. A field trip can be a rewarding experience, but it can also be a costly one should an accident occur and the teacher be found negligent.

Locker and Personal Searches

Courts have rendered a variety of decisions relative to locker and personal searches of students. The preponderance of legal precedent leads us to conclude that for *just cause* teachers or school administrators may search student lockers, even though students rent the locker or put their own lock on the locker.

Just cause has been defined as a reasonable suspicion that the student is hiding contraband, controlled substances, or weapons. Some courts have recently ruled that in the presence of just cause students' Fourth Amendment constitutional rights have not been violated. Reasonableness is the criterion courts use when dealing with cases relating to this issue. Necessary actions taken by school personnel to provide a safe environment, conducive to learning, are generally supported by the courts.

It strengthens the case, should a lawsuit arise as the result of a locker search, if the school maintains a master list of locker combinations or a master key, thus conveying the idea that the lockers belong to the school rather than to the student.

Generally speaking, the evidence gained in a locker search without a search warrant is not admissible in court. The courts seem quite concerned about protecting the student's Fourth Amendment rights if the result of a locker search is to be utilized for anything beyond school discipline. Students have a reasonable expectation of privacy.

If school personnel decide to inspect a locker and use whatever is found in the locker as the basis for pressing charges against the student, then the locker should only be opened with a proper search warrant. Once the warrant is obtained, the parent should be informed and offered the opportunity to be present, with legal counsel, at the locker opening. In addition, no outsiders, such as police officers, should be allowed to open a student's locker without a warrant and without prior parent notification. Generally courts have ruled that if a school agent opens a student locker at police request but without a warrant, any evidence found in the locker is inadmissible in court.

Search of a student's person usually takes the form of the student being requested to empty his pockets or, in cases involving a female, to empty her purse. The above guidelines relating to locker searches generally apply in these cases. Some courts have ruled that the school agent stands *in loco parentis* and thus personal searches are constitutional. Other courts have ruled that, because of the authority relationship between a teacher and a student, the student has no choice but to empty pockets or purse when told to do so, and thus the evidence was gained under duress.

In summary, legal precedent affirms the right of school personnel to search lockers and students for just cause and subsequently to administer school discipline if warranted. However, evidence found in such searches and used to press charges may be inadmissible in court if not obtained by a search warrant.

Discipline

Teachers have always used a variety of methods to enforce discipline and to punish recalcitrants. This section deals with four methods that could have legal ramifications. For more detailed information, see fastback 121 *Student Discipline and the Law*.

Corporal Punishment

Generally, due process procedures are not required before administering corporal punishment. The U.S. Supreme Court has also ruled that, in the absence of a state law or school district policy that prohibits corporal punishment, administration of corporal punishment does not violate a student's constitutional rights. However, the teacher must be certain that the student understands, prior to the punishment, that certain behaviors or breaches of school rules could result in corporal punishment. Thus, an informal due process hearing may be needed to ensure that students understand the consequences of their actions. We suggest that if corporal punishment is to be a disciplinary consequence, the teacher present to the students a written list of the types of student actions that could result in corporal punishment.

Teachers also should remember that state laws and school board policies that permit corporal punishment often contain restrictions. For example, some policies or laws state that if parents submit a statement in writing to the school superintendent indicating that they do not want corporal punishment administered to their children, then such punishment cannot be used. The teacher should check with the principal about pertinent state law or school board policy before administering corporal punishment.

Finally, the teacher must recognize that corporal punishment can be interpreted as other actions besides spanking, slapping, or paddling. Putting a student in a dark closet, making a student do an excessive number of push-ups in a gym class for forgetting his gym clothes, or making a student stand on his tip-toes with his nose in a circle drawn on a blackboard could cause physical or emotional harm to a student and may be interpreted as forms of corporal punishment. Such interpretations present grounds for legal action where state law or school board policy prohibits corporal punishment.

Mass Punishment

Sometimes an incident occurs in a classroom and the teacher does not know which student did it. For example, someone strikes a match and the teacher smells the fumes but cannot determine who lit the match. Most teachers will first attempt to have the guilty student admit his behavior. If this effort fails, the teacher then may ask other class members to identify the guilty student. If this fails, the teacher may discipline the entire class by denying privileges, keeping the class after school or in from recess, or making the class perform tedious tasks such as a long list of math problems. Experience has shown that none of these mass punishments will be supported by the courts since the innocent are punished along with the guilty.

After-School Detention

Another form of discipline frequently used by teachers is detaining the misbehaving student after school. While such a practice may be an effective disciplinary measure, it does present some legal concerns. First, the student kept after school must be under the supervision of the teacher or some other responsible adult. Second, by keeping a student after school the teacher may cause the student who is bused to miss the bus home. If the student then walks home, crosses busy streets with no crossing guards present, and is involved in an accident, the teacher who kept the student after school may be found liable for the accident.

If a teacher does use after-school detention, the parent should be notified in writing specifying when the student will be kept after school and informing the parent that he is responsible for providing safe transportation home. The parent should be asked to sign the statement and return it to the teacher on the day the detention will occur. In the absence of a signed form, the student should be disciplined by other means than after-school detention. The teacher should not rely on a phone call to communicate disciplinary action to the parent.

Discipline and Grades

Can grades be lowered for poor deportment? Decisions rendered in New Jersey and Ohio held that grades could not be lowered for disciplinary reasons. Yet in Illinois and Texas, courts have ruled to the contrary. Our suggestion is that the teacher make it very clear to the students at the beginning of the course and in writing the criteria used for awarding final grades. If deportment is included, the specific manner in which deportment affects the final grade should be stated. In schools that use a grading system with one grade for academic achievement and another for deportment, the academic achievement grade should not be negatively affected by poor deportment. As a general guideline, the more informed students are about how their grades will be determined the less likely a teacher will be sued for giving a poor grade.

Trespass of Personal Property

It is common practice for teachers to take water guns from students and destroy them or throw them in waste baskets or to take comic books or girlie magazines from students and tear them to shreds. Teachers should realize that these items are the students' personal property and they have no right to destroy them. Of course, teachers can have rules that prohibit bringing items into the classroom that are unsafe or distractions and can take them from students if brought to class. However, the teacher should have a procedure for returning these items to the student. Items can be returned at the end of the day, at the end of the semester, or to a parent who is requested to come to school.

The exception to the above suggestion is bringing dangerous weapons or controlled substances into the classroom. These items may be permanently confiscated. Obvious dangerous weapons are knives, guns, and chains; but a nail file in the hand of a student who is jabbing another student is also a dangerous weapon and may be confiscated.

Teachers may not think they can be sued for trespass of personal property for something as trivial as tearing up a comic book. But it has happened. Typically, these suits ask for punitive damages because the teacher embarrassed the student, causing emotional trauma because of teasing from peers. Some lower courts have found for the student in such cases. Suits of this type are easily avoided. All the teacher has to do is set rules for classroom behavior and enforce them. If violation of the rules occurs and items are taken from students, have a policy for returning the items to the student at a later date.

Supervision and Liability

T he school code in most states specifies that the building principal is responsible for the safety and well-being of students while at school. Thus, when principals assign teachers such supervisory duties as bus loading and unloading, restroom supervision, hallway monitoring, lunch room supervision, and supervision of extracurricular activities, they are fulfilling their legal mandate. In absence of contractual language to the contrary and as long as the teachers are not assigned supervisory responsibilities in a discriminatory fashion, the principal has the right to ask teachers to assist in supervising student behavior.

While teachers' primary responsibility is to ensure the safety and well-being of the students in their own classrooms or work stations, they also carry some responsibility for supervision throughout the building. If a teacher observes a student doing something that is potentially harmful to self or others, such as running in a hallway or lighting a match in the restroom, the teacher must take steps to stop the student. If a student is injured and it could be proven that the teacher made no effort to stop the student, the teacher could be held liable for an act of omission.

There have been a number of court cases in which a student was injured while the teacher was absent from the classroom. In these cases, the courts have attempted to ascertain if the teacher's absence from the classroom constituted a *proximate cause* of the injury; that is, did the teacher's absence directly contribute to the injury? Proximate cause usually relates to the teacher's foreknowledge that an injury might occur. For example, if a teacher leaves two students alone who have a history of fighting and one student is injured, a court might rule that the teacher should have known that being absent from the classroom might be the occasion for a fight.

When considering whether a teacher is liable for a student injury while the teacher is absent from the classroom, the courts also consider the length of time the teacher was away from the classroom, the reason for the teacher's absence, the maturity and mental capacities of the students, and the nature of the classroom activity. Obviously, the degree of care needed in supervising a science laboratory, gymnasium, home economics room, or shop class is greater than in a history or English class.

While proximate cause is difficult to prove and teachers generally have not been found liable for injuries sustained during their absence, the prudent teacher does not take chances. Students should not be left unsupervised.

In addition, teachers who conduct such after-school activities as play rehearsal, band practice, club meetings, and sports practices must provide the same care and supervision as they would during the school day. An after-school activity should not be left to the supervision of a student, such as a club president.

Our guideline here can best be summarized in two words, reasonableness and prudence. The teacher must provide that amount and kind of care that a reasonable and prudent parent would provide under similar circumstances.

Insurance and Liability

No discussion of legal basics for teachers should conclude without some consideration of insurance, particulary liability insurance. There are four types of insurance with which teachers should be familiar: malpractice insurance, tort liability insurance, automobile insurance, and personal possessions insurance.

Malpractice Insurance

Teachers may read about a physician who had to pay thousands of dollars because of medical malpractice and think that they should indemnify themselves by purchasing malpractice insurance. And there are plenty of companies eager to sell them. We urge caution. While there have been some court cases charging teachers and their school systems with malpractice because a student did not learn, no teacher to date has ever lost a malpractice suit. By definition, malpractice means that a person does not perform his or her job according to commonly accepted standards of the profession. In teaching, such standards are hard to pin down. Generally, courts have taken the position that teachers are responsible for providing the opportunity to learn but cannot be held liable for a student's lack of achievement. The courts' posture seems to recognize that there are external factors affecting achievement over which the teacher has no control, such as a deprived home environment.

A second argument for teachers not purchasing malpractice insurance is that such purchase, in a sense, is tantamount to admitting that the teacher could be guilty of malpractice. Why indemnify oneself for an action for which one cannot be held liable? However, keep in mind that even though teachers have not been found guilty of malpractice, they can be, and have been, dismissed for incompetency.

Tort Liability Insurance

Teachers need tort liability insurance in the event that a negligence suit is filed as the result of a student being injured at school or a school-related activity. In many states there are laws that require the school board to indemnify its teachers against tort action. Also, membership in a professional association such as the National Education Association or its state affiliate includes some liability coverage. In addition, teachers can purchase liability insurance from private insurance companies, usually at a quite reasonable annual premium.

Automobile Insurance

Most teachers, coaches, and administrators do not carry enough automobile liability insurance to be transporting children for school activities in their personal automobile. If an accident occurs and the teacher is found negligent, the standard liability coverage for a personal automobile is not likely to be sufficient, and the teacher could be forced to pay damages from personal assets. In smaller schools, teachers and coaches sometimes find it necessary to transport small groups such as cheerleaders, golf teams, debate teams, or tennis teams in their own automobiles. In such situations, where no school district transportation is available, the teacher should insist the school board indemnify the teacher before agreeing to such transportation arrangements.

Insurance for Personal Possessions

In schools where funds are limited, dedicated teachers often will bring their personal record players, cassette recorders, and other audiovisual equipment to use in class. If a student damages or steals the equipment, frequently school district insurance policies do not cover the teacher's personal property. Even in cases where the district's policy does cover teachers' property, the loss must be a result of forced entry; that is, the classroom, the teacher's desk, or storage cabinet must be forcibly entered. Forced entry may be difficult to prove if the property is stolen when the teacher is on hall patrol, at the principal's office, or at the nurse's office. Teachers should check the district's insurance coverage before bringing personal items to school. In the absence of district coverage teachers might check their homeowner's policy to see if coverage of stolen property is restricted by the forced-entry clause.

Bibliography

Alexander, K. *School Law*. St. Paul, Minn.: West, 1980.

Connors, Eugene T. *Educational Tort Liability and Malpractice*. Bloomington, Ind.: Phi Delta Kappa, 1981.

Connors, E.T. *Student Discipline and the Law*. Fastback 121. Bloomington,
Ind.: Phi Delta Kappa Educational Foundation, 1979.

Fisher, L.; Schimmel, D.; and Kelly, C. *Teachers and the Law*. New York:
Longman, 1981.

Hazard, W.R. *Education and the Law: Cases and Materials on Public Schools*.
2nd ed. New York: Free Press, 1978.

Kemerer, F.R., and Deutsch, K.L. *Constitutional Rights and Student Life*.
St. Paul, Minn.: West, 1979.

London, S.B., and Stile, S.W. *The School's Role in the Prevention of Child
Abuse*. Fastback 172. Bloomington, Ind.: Phi Delta Kappa Educational
Foundation, 1982.

Memin, S. *Law and the Legal System: An Introduction*. Boston: Little, Brown,
1973.

Morris, A.A. *The Constitution and American Education*. St. Paul, Minn.:
West, 1980.

Reutter, E.E., Jr., and Hamilton, R.H. *The Law and Public Education*. 2nd
ed. New York: Foundation Press, 1976.

Valente, W. *Law in the Schools*. Columbus, Ohio: Bell and Howell, Charles
E. Merrill, 1980.